TWO GOOD ROUNDS

TWO GOOD ROUNDS
19th Hole Stories from the World's Greatest Golfers

ELISA GAUDET

SKYHORSE PUBLISHING

Skyhorse Publishing books may be purchased in bulk at special discounts for sales promotion, corporate gifts, fund-raising, or educational purposes. Special editions can also be created to specifications. For details, contact the Special Sales Department, Skyhorse Publishing, 307 West 36th Street, 11th Floor, New York, NY 10018 or info@skyhorsepublishing.com.

Skyhorse® and Skyhorse Publishing® are registered trademarks of Skyhorse Publishing, Inc.®, a Delaware corporation.

Visit our website at www.skyhorsepublishing.com.

10 9 8 7 6 5 4 3 2 1

Two Good Rounds logo design by Monica Nossa

Library of Congress Cataloging-in-Publication Data available on file.

ISBN: 978-1-61608-641-1

Printed in China

Contents

In Palm Beach with legends Gary Player (L) and Seve Ballesteros (R).

The reason there are eighteen holes on a golf course is because there are eighteen shots in a bottle of whiskey and when the bottle was empty the round was done.

— Golf folklore

Golf is very much like a love affair. If you don't take it seriously, it's no fun, but if you do, it breaks your heart. Don't break your heart, but flirt with the possibility.

— Louise Suggs

I miss. I miss. I make.

— Seve Ballesteros, describing his four-putt at Augusta's No. 16 in 1988

Masters 2008

Jack Nicklaus and his son, Jack Nicklaus II walking the Masters course.

Corey Pavin and I with the Ryder Cup

Introduction

Life is at its best when it's shaken and stirred! Everybody loves a celebration and golfers are no exception. It has long been a tradition after a round of golf to gather together and celebrate a win or merely enjoy the company of friends, new and old, with a second round at the 19th hole.

Outside The 19th Hole in Cape Cod.

The 19th hole is a slang term used in golf that refers to a pub, bar, or restaurant on or near the golf course. A standard round of golf has only eighteen holes, so golfers will say they are at the "nineteenth hole," meaning they are enjoying a drink after their round. Golf courses have always been a place to connect with nature and with friends. If it were not for the 19th hole there would be no place to connect the dots between golf, nature, and all those marvelous tales of eagles and birdies.

Golf is an international sport that continues to travel and touch more people in more countries than ever before. Being reinstated into the Olympics exemplifies its global reach.

Two Good Rounds is therefore an international tribute to great golfers around the world in which they reveal in their own words their momentous wins, their most memorable golf stories, their favorite drinks, and other entertaining aspects of the golf lifestyle.

Miacomet Golf Club's John Daly

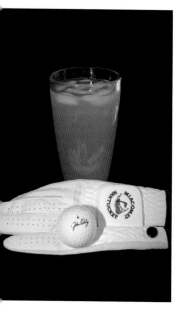

While working in the golf industry over the years I have met the most interesting people, made terrific business contacts, and developed great story ideas at the 19th hole. "On the Lip," a golf column I have been writing since 2003, was an idea scribbled on a cocktail napkin one day while having drinks in Miami with a longtime golf friend, Walt Shuler. Working on the business side of the golf industry for both the PGA Tour and the Latin golf tour, Tour de las Américas, and writing the "OTL" column have afforded me the opportunity to get to know a number of professional tour players. While vacationing on Nantucket Island I noticed a drink called the "John Daly" (iced tea, lemonade, and vodka) on the menu at the Miacomet Golf Club.

I was thinking of writing a column on Nantucket, golf, and the drink but instead it became the inspiration for this book.

While I have a great deal of respect for my fellow golf journalists and their work covering tournament golf, I have chosen to write about the lighter side of the game. As my good friend George Willis from the **New York Post** jokingly put it, "Elisa writes a fluff column." Sometimes we all need a little fluff, a good laugh, and a reminder to not take ourselves too seriously. It is my hope that this book will highlight, in a respectful manner, the lifestyle and lighter side of golf that we all enjoy and also provide interesting vignettes of Tour pros doing the same. It is worth mentioning, however, the importance of drinking responsibly. Perhaps Fuzzy Zoeller said it best on his Fuzzy Vodka website, where he wrote, "Trust your caddie and please drink responsibly."

After attending the Metropolitan Golf Writers Dinner in 2009, a few of us gathered at the hotel bar for drinks. One special man

The King and I

in attendance was Arnold Palmer. To be able to spend a little time socializing with The King off the golf course and in a relaxed environment while enjoying a drink was a very special moment for me and one of my all-time favorite experiences at the 19th hole. The fact that we both enjoy vodka just exemplifies that I am one step closer to being a better golfer.

One of the most spectacular 19th holes is the outside bar at the Inn at Spanish Bay in Pebble Beach where every day at sunset a bagpiper closes the course in Scottish tradition. The grill room at Isleworth is beyond one's imagination during the Tavistock Cup, with the Tour players relaxing and playing pinball and half-court basketball or using the golf simulator—all of which are inside the grill room. This is what a fifteen-year-old boy would design if he had $20 million. The bar at Winged Foot is a treat, and the cocktail areas where people sit and enjoy a drink before going into dinner are bursting with golf memorabilia from the legends that have walked the club's fairways over the years. The bar at Port Royal Golf Club in Bermuda is perched above the golf course and has breathtaking views of the bluest ocean you have ever seen. The Dark and Stormy and Rum Swizzles taste just a little bit better from there.

By far my most jubilant 19th hole memories stem from attending the last seven Masters tournaments. The first year I attended the Masters was with a ticket given to me by Seve Ballesteros as a birthday gift. Sitting on the lawn at Augusta National, inside the ropes in the clubhouse lunch area, sipping the club's famous Azalea cocktail (one part lime or lemon juice, one part canned pineapple juice, three parts gin, grenadine to color pink, mixed in a cocktail shaker and shaken with ice) provides a perfect 19th hole moment. The day and evening hospitality events in Augusta are teeming with interesting people and celebrities. The Marquis Jet and NetJets folks throw some of the best parties, and over the years they never cease to amaze me with their impeccably detailed hospitality and creativity. The bar at the Partridge Inn in Augusta has always been a favorite during the week of the Masters, as it is a great place to meet friends old and new and a place where many golf writers get together. I have fond memories of enjoying drinks, smoking cigars on the porch, talking golf until the wee hours, singing, and even

16th Stadium Hole
—WM Phoenix Open

meeting an Irish prime minister—well, at least that's who I was told

he was.

In the spirit of writing a book about golf and drinks I felt it was my obligation to visit the PGA Tour event known for being the largest golf party in the world. The Waste Management Phoenix Open, hosted by the Thunderbirds, has raised more than $70 million for charities and holds the record for drawing the largest crowds for any golfing event in the world. The tournament has gained legendary status for being a unique stop on the PGA Tour,

INTRODUCTION

Australia's Ian Baker-Finch kissing the Claret Jug after winning the 1991 Open Championship

where the activities and party environment off the fairways are often more popular than the golf. The famed 16th hole, a challenging par 3, puts players to the test, and the stadium seating on that hole alone holds anywhere from 12,000 to 15,000 people. The tournament has hosted crowds as large as 538,000 for the week. Thunderbirds are big fans of Pabst Blue Ribbon and perhaps it is a secret ingredient in their beer dogs, which are sold at the event. The Thunderbird organization and the tournament staff pull out all the stops to ensure people have a good time.

Some of the best trophies in the world are the ones you can drink from, the big silver cups. Golf being no exception, the trophy awarded to the winner of The Open Championship (or British Open) is officially known as the Championship Cup, but it is much more commonly called the "Claret Jug" because that's what it actually is. Claret is a dry red wine produced in the famous French winemaking region of Bordeaux. The British Open trophy was made in the style of silver jugs used to serve claret at nineteenth-century gatherings.

The PGA Championship's Wannamaker Trophy is another example of a great cup trophy. As it turns out the top does come off, and I was told I would have to ask past PGA champions what they have sipped from the trophy. Interestingly, the Ryder Cup is the smallest of the trophies and must be shared by 12 guys. I assume they would need to use straws.

No one can appreciate a good cup trophy and the taste of success better than Rory McIlroy, the U.S. Open champ who took to Twitter to share his joy in winning the U.S. Open in 2011. "Tastes good!!!" tweeted McIlroy when he posted a picture of himself drinking from the U.S. Open Trophy. McIlroy has listed Jägermeister and Heineken as his adult beverages of choice. Other champions before him, Graeme McDowell and Michael Campbell, have also revealed in our interviews that they too have also experienced moments of celebration drinking from the U.S. Open Trophy.

Chubby Chandler, the agent for Tour pros Ernie Els, Darren Clarke, Lee Westwood, Rory McIlroy, and Louis

Enjoying a beverage with 2010 U.S. Open champion Graeme McDowell

Oosthuizen, has been known to take over the Jigger Inn, a watering hole situated on the end of the Old Course Hotel and beside the seventeenth, the famous Road Hole, during The Open. "We have players and their families and a few friends over in the evening, people from all over the world and some of the lads who are staying at the Old Course hotel," Chandler says of his haven.

For the book *Two Good Rounds*, I asked each of the thirty-six players interviewed the same questions: What is your favorite drink? What is your favorite clubhouse or 19th hole? And what is a special time or memory from a 19th hole? I also asked if they ever made a hole in one, if so how many, and if they bought the clubhouse a round. What I received were myriad answers ranging from crazy celebrations after a win to heartfelt memories as a child growing up playing golf with family and friends. I hope you will enjoy this book over a pint, a shot of vodka, a glass of chardonnay, an Arnold Palmer, or a tall glass of milk with Oreos. Cheers!

Chubby Chandler outside the Jigger Inn

US Open Trophy

Dallas Cowboys
quarterback and avid
golfer Tony Romo

At the 19th
Hole at the WM
Phoenix Open

TWO GOOD ROUNDS

Arnold Palmer
United States

The King of golf has long had a drink named after him. The "Half and Half," half unsweetened iced tea and half lemonade, is better known as the Arnold Palmer. It's no surprise that this is Arnold's favorite drink even today. The evolution of this relatively simple concoction that he first asked for in Palm Springs, California, in the early 1960s has now become a popular staple at golf clubs and restaurants across the globe. Because of its popularity, a number of Arnold Palmer variations have been developed after the "Half and Half" as a result of a licensing arrangement with Arizona Beverage Company.

Arnold enjoys a Ketel One on the rocks when he is having a cocktail. When asked if he is aware of a drink known as the John Daly (lemonade, iced tea, and vodka), he replied, "Well, young lady, I like an Arnold Palmer with Ketel One—an Arnold Palmer with a kick."

Arnold Palmer had created an impressive and successful golf course–design business with over 300 courses in 28 countries. When asked why there are 18 holes on a golf course, Arnold replied, "According to legend, that's what it takes to finish a bottle of scotch.

FAVORITE DRINK

A classic Arnold Palmer, one-half lemonade, one-half iced tea

19TH HOLE "I have two favorite spots where I prefer to spend my time after a round," Palmer said. "Latrobe Country Club and Bay Hill." Palmer splits his time, spending his summers in Latrobe, Pennsylvania, and his winters at Bay Hill in Orlando, Florida. "Golf has been a large part of my life and I have always enjoyed sharing special moments with friends and family after a round over drinks or a Half and Half."

The Latrobe Country Club is his home course, where at the age of four he first started swinging a golf club. His father, Milfred (Deacon) Palmer, worked at the Latrobe Country Club from 1921 until his death in 1976 as a golf professional and course superintendent. Palmer caddied at the club and worked almost every other possible job at the club as well. "This is where I go to gather with the guys, my friends, and we talk and have a couple of drinks with pretzels and potato chips."

The Mixed Grille is located upstairs in the Clubhouse at the Latrobe Country Club and is the primary dining room. Along with some unique items on the menu like duck, venison, and ostrich, you'll also find many of Mr. Palmer's favorites, like Palmer crab cakes and Palmer mashed potatoes, which are mashed potatoes with horseradish and scallions.

There is an overwhelming amount of Palmer memorabilia covering the walls, including hundreds of photos of Arnold with presidents, royalty, and celebrities.

Arnold Palmer has met every US president from Eisenhower to Obama and often played golf with Eisenhower, who regularly shot in the low 80s. "I spent a lot of time with Ike talking and golfing," Palmer said. "I have played with Ford, Bush forty-one, and was on my way to play with Kennedy in Palm Beach when he hurt his back."

When at Bay Hill Palmer prefers the men's locker room because "it is a friendly place where we play cards, chat about our round, and compare scorecards." The Bay Hill men's locker room is also a favorite among many Tour players.

The first win he celebrated was the 1955 Canadian Open. After he won Arnold, his wife, Winnie, and Tommy Bolt had dinner and drinks at a cottage near the clubhouse. "After I won the British Open at Royal Birkdale I received a call from Walter Hagen. That was a surprise and thrill for me."

HOLES IN ONE

Arnold has made nineteen holes in one and recalled two of his favorites. "Probably the craziest thing that has happened regarding a hole in one was during a tournament at TPC Avenel in Washington, DC, on September 2, 1986, when I got a hole in one on the third hole. NBC was covering the tournament at the time and the next day they showed up on the third hole. When I asked what they were doing there they said they were coming to film the hole in one I was about to make. I thought they were crazy but sure enough I got a hole in one on the same hole as the day before. Two days in a row I got a hole in one on the same hole, number three; there is a plaque on the hole.

"I was playing Bay Hill and on the seventeenth hole my caddy gave me a club that I told him was not the right club. He insisted it was and I proceeded to hit the ball into the water. At this point I decided to hit another ball from the tee and take the penalty. This time I took the club I thought I should use and it went on the green and rolled in for a hole in one. I looked at the caddy and said, 'See, this is the right club.' The caddy turned to me and said, 'No, you hit that fat.'"

ARNIE'S ARMY   When asked if he had the opportunity to do any shots over what comes to mind, he chuckled and responded, "Oh, there are a lot of shots I would do over . . . the Open at Olympic, the Masters, Oakmont in 1962 come to mind quickly."

Nowadays we are inundated with media images and we are able to see and hear from superstar athletes via Facebook and Twitter. It is interesting to look back to an earlier era without technology and realize how organic and widespread Arnold Palmer's mass appeal was. He attributes this to the fact that he likes people and always appreciated that they rooted for him so hard. When having a drink at the 19th hole he always made time to talk to people and sign autographs.

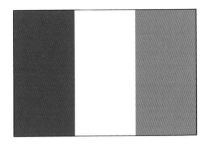

Padraig Harrington
Ireland

Harrington has won three major championships: The Open Championship in 2007 and 2008 and the PGA Championship, also in 2008. Rather than drinking some stout or lager from the cup to celebrate, as some might think he would, his son Patrick had another idea. After Harrington's Open win in 2007, Patrick was caught on microphone asking his father if they could "put ladybirds in it" (referring to the trophy). Following his win in 2008, there were some lighthearted references to this in a subsequent interview, whereupon Harrington suggested that it was more likely that Patrick would now want to put snails in the trophy.

While most Irishmen enjoy a good pint, Coca-Cola (actually Diet Coke) is Harrington's favorite drink.

FAVORITE DRINK

Harrington's favorite grill room is at Royal Dublin Golf Club. "I love the Spike Bar in Royal Dublin Golf Club," he said. "It's very small so there is always a good atmosphere, and being so enclosed makes it a very warm and enjoyable place to be on a cold winter's day."

19TH HOLE

Harrington estimates that he has made around a dozen holes in one. "My most important was in my last amateur tournament at the

HOLES IN ONE

Malahide Golf Club in Dublin, Ireland, while playing in the All Ireland Mother and Son Championship," he said. "We won by half a shot!" Despite their jubilation, the Harringtons did not buy the clubhouse a shot afterwards.

Did You Know?

Prior to turning pro, Harrington mixed amateur golf with studying for an accounting degree and passed his final exams in 1994 to gain admittance to ACCA (Association of Chartered Certified Accountants).

TWO GOOD ROUNDS

Darren Clarke
Northern Ireland

"My favorite drink is Guinness," the 2011 Open champion said, "and I do like lots and lots and lots of it. I also like champagne sometimes, and my country is famous for our Irish whiskey. Bushmills distillery, the most famous Irish whiskey, is three miles from where I live." When asked if there was a drink that tastes better after a win, Clarke said, "The amount of Guinness increases after a win, but it still tastes the same."

FAVORITE DRINK

Clarke's favorite 19th hole is a little bar in Portrush, Ireland, at the harbour, called the Harbour Bar. "Harbour Bar is said to be the oldest pub in Northern Ireland," Clarke said. "The Guinness tastes the best there. There is a difference and some important factors are how much the bar sells and if the pipes are clean. Also Guinness does not travel well. It is always best at home.

19TH HOLE

"I won my first professional tournament in 1993 in Belgium, the Alfred Dunhill Open. Ten minutes after I won I called back home to the golf course that is my home course, Dungannon Golf Club in Northern Ireland, and told the clubhouse that [for] anyone that was in the bar, the drinks were on me. All I know is when I got the bill it was clear they drank a lot."

HOLES IN ONE When recounting his most memorable holes in one, Clarke said, "The sixteenth hole at Dungannon Golf Club was a good one. However I have never won a car or prize. I seem to always make the holes in one on the wrong holes.

BUYING THE CLUBHOUSE A DRINK "I frequently buy rounds of drinks," Clarke said. "I have no problem putting my hand in [my] pocket to buy people drinks. Mr. [Lee] Westwood, Mr. [Ernie] Els, and I have enjoyed a cocktail now and again."

The Oldest Distillery in Ireland

It was in 1608 that King James I granted the Bushmills region of Ireland an official license to distill, but Bushmills's notoriety has been thought to go back a few centuries prior, with tales of King Henry II's troops imbibing its spirits. The tradition is alive at the oldest operating distillery in Ireland, where the entire process, from distillation to bottling, takes place. Over the last 400 years Bushmills has developed a name worldwide as a fine example of classic Irish whiskey.

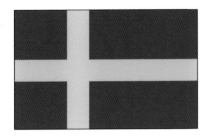

Annika Sörenstam
Sweden

Annika Sörenstam has won ninety-three international tournaments as a professional, making her the female golfer with the most wins to her name. She has won seventy-two official LPGA tournaments including ten majors and eighteen other tournaments internationally. Sörenstam made history at the Bank of America Colonial tournament in 2003 when she became the first woman to play in a men's PGA Tour event since 1945.

FAVORITE DRINK

"I enjoy drinking wine and red more than white," Sörenstam said. "At first when I was trying wines it was either red or white. Now I can distinguish and complement different wines with different foods."

The grapes for Annika's signature wine are grown and vinified based on a family winemaking tradition that dates back five generations to 1883. The Wente Vineyards in Livermore Valley, California, produce the Annika Syrah and the Annika Chardonnay. "We produce premium reds that are not mass produced," Sörenstam said. "A great thing about Wente Vineyards is that they have wine, [plus] 9 and dine events right there at the vineyard as there is a nine-hole course on the property.

19TH HOLE "The Tap Room at Pebble Beach has always been a favorite because of the fun atmosphere, and I have very fond memories of celebrating [there] after the Solheim Cup," Sörenstam said. "Also, I recall after my U.S. Open win in 1995 I drank champagne out of the trophy.

"Probably my fondest memories as a child are those spent in the summer growing up on the Bro-Bålsta Golf Club in Stockholm, Sweden. My parents would play golf and pull my sister and I around on their pull carts and take us for a vanilla ice cream after the round. We would get golf balls from the water and have putting contests. It was very much a family atmosphere on the weekends and my friends, my sister, and I would dive in the lakes for golf balls and pick up balls on the range for money. Junior golfers were very welcome at the club. We had our own room called the junior corner where there was always music and we would hang out.

"I have made four," Sörenstam said. "The first was when I was sixteen or seventeen years old in Stockholm on the seventh hole. I remember winning a head cover from the club house."

HOLES IN ONE

Graeme McDowell
Northern Ireland

"I enjoy drinking Guinness beer when I am in Ireland and when I can get it," McDowell said. "Otherwise I enjoy a light lager, red wine, or Coors Light.

"My favorite 19th hole would be the bar at my home course, Rathmore Golf Club in Portrush, Ireland," McDowell said. "I have always enjoyed and still do enjoy sitting around with my dad, brothers, and friends after a round of golf.

"When in the states I enjoy going to the Lake Nona grill room for a drink with the boys after a round and socializing." After the

McDowell (far left) celebrating the 2011 Tavistock Cup championships with his Lake Nona teammates Ross Fisher, Retief Goosen, Peter Hanson, Henrik Stenson, and Oliver Wilson

Lake Nona team won the 2011 Tavistock Cup, Graeme announced, "The thing about the Lake Nona team is we probably party the best. We will probably have a few beers after this."

McDowell, the 2010 U.S. Open champion, celebrated the win in Carmel, California.

"After the U.S. Open win at Pebble Beach we all went to an old-school Irish bar in Carmel near Pebble called Brophy's Tavern," McDowell said. "I was with my family and friends and I may have been the drunkest man on earth.

"The next day I woke up and saw the trophy on the table in my room and thought, *this is a really great hangover*. I had to pinch myself. When I went back to Ireland we had a party at my golf club, Rathmore, and we did drink lager out of the trophy cup. Another fun moment and celebration was after the 2010 Ryder Cup win, Rory McIlroy and I did Jägermeister bombs out of the Ryder Cup. I really enjoy the social aspect of getting together with fifteen to twenty school friends and relaxing in the clubhouse at Christmas time and when I am home, which isn't as often since I travel so much.

"When I can I fly with Marquis Jet, Sunday is 'bevi night,' "McDowell said. "Nothing crazy, but we just finished a tournament and [when we're] in the air going to another location I will sometimes enjoy a beer. I remember flying back from Korea with Ernie [Els] after a tournament and he wasn't happy with his performance so the first half of the flight was pretty quiet. The second half we managed to have a chat over a beer."

HOLES IN ONE   McDowell estimates that he has made eight holes in one in his lifetime. "The most memorable [one] was in Denmark during the

Carlsberg Nordic Open in 2003," he said. "I was on the cut line and on the fourteenth hole I got a hole in one [from] two hundred and twenty yards using a 3-iron. I made the cut and won an Audi. Afterwards, I went into the clubhouse members' lounge and I bought a round for the members."

Martin Laird
Scotland

"Irn-Bru is my favorite drink and probably the national drink of Scotland," Laird said. "Irn-Bru is a carbonated soft drink produced in Westfield, Cumbernauld, Scotland. It is also Scottish folklore but a bottle of cold Irn-Bru is said to be the day-after cure for headaches after you have had a few too many drinks."

Innovative and sometimes controversial marketing campaigns have kept it as one of the best-selling soft drinks in Scotland, where it competes directly with global brands such as Coca-Cola and Pepsi. Scotland is the only country in the world where

FAVORITE DRINK

Coca-Cola sales are not the highest in the soft-drink market, as Irn-Bru is currently the most popular soft-drink.

It is thought that the name Irn-Bru originated with the re-building of Glasgow Central Station in 1901. When workers from the William Beardmore and Company steelworks in Glasgow were dying from the large amounts of beer drunk to quench their thirst from the heat of the steelworks, an alternative was sought. A local soft-drinks manufacturer, A.G. Barr, approached the steelworks and a contract was created to provide the workers with this drink. This unnamed drink later went on to be known as "Iron Brew" because of its connections to the steel- (and iron-) works.

"After playing golf with my Dad I really enjoy having a Cale-donian 80 beer," Laird said. Beer in Scotland was traditionally cat-egorized in shillings by the amount of tax charged per 504-pint barrel (called a hogshead):

40/- ale was a very light beer often supplied to farmhands.

50/- and 60/- beers were also reasonably light and mild.

70/-, 80/-, and 90/- were progressively stronger, export-quality beers.

The shilling terminology continued to be used to indicate the beers' quality and the system was legally recognized in 1914.

19TH HOLE "I grew up playing golf at Hilton Park Golf Club in Milngavie, Glasgow, Scotland," Laird said, "and the best 19th hole for me is the 'Dirty Bar' at my club. It is called the 'Dirty Bar' because you can wear your spikes in the bar. When I was playing as a junior golfer I could not go in because you have to be eighteen. I grew up playing with my dad and now when I am back [in Glasgow] he and I go there for lunch and a beer after a round.

Justin Timberlake on the course

"One of my favorite moments or 19th hole celebrations was after my Nationwide [Tour] win in Athens, Georgia," Laird said. "We had already planned to go to the Killers concert on Sunday night. It was my first big win and we had dinner and went to the concert. They are one of my favorite bands so it was a fun way to celebrate."

HOLES IN ONE

Laird has made three holes in one. "The first was most memorable," he said, "because I was playing on my home course with a good friend for a couple of bucks which was a big deal in those days. On seventeen I got a hole in one to close out the match but my friend refused to pay me because he was mad. I wasn't old enough to go in the bar so I did not have to buy the clubhouse a round. I still tease him about not paying me for that round.

"The second hole in one I got was in Arizona when I was playing with three friends. It was on the nineth or tenth hole when I got the hole in one and as I looked up the beer cart was fifty yards away. It was told to stay with us the rest of the round and I had to buy drinks.

FIRST PGA TOUR WIN

"After my win at the Justin Timberlake Shriners Open in 2009 I met Justin at the awards ceremony, which was very cool given [the tournament] was being played in Las Vegas," Laird said. "The Saturday night before I was in contention, and we all went to the concert Justin does every year. It was a good way to take my mind off golf. A really great treat was that since it was my first PGA Tour win my fiancée, manager, friend, and I all stayed at the Hard Rock Hotel and Casino, which was also very appropriate given we were in Las Vegas. We stayed in an amazing suite and had dinner and drinks there. They also sent us a nice bottle of champagne."

Arnie's Influence

"I never met Arnold Palmer until I came up the eighteenth green in 2011 for my win at the Bay Hill Invitational. The funny thing is the first set of irons I ever had when I was five years old were Arnold Palmer irons. When I first came to the USA to play college golf at Colorado State University, I tried an Arnold Palmer drink and have been hooked [on them] ever since."

Martin Laird has been a member of Arnie's Army since he was five years old.

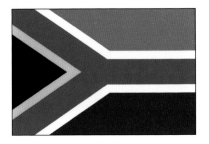

Gary Player
South Africa

"My favorite recipe is for the drink I have each morning," Player said. "It is hard to get when I am traveling, but at home I drink this every day":

FAVORITE DRINK

- 2 spinach leaves
- 1 kale leaf
- Juice of one half lemon
- Small piece ginger
- 1 apple
- 1/2 cucumber
- 1 piece celery
- Combine ingredients in a juicer and drink immediately

"The first time I met Ben Hogan was in the locker room at the 1958 U.S. Open at Southern Hills Country Club in Tulsa, Oklahoma," Player said. "Hogan was a very intimidating person and not easy to approach, but I shook his hand and told him it was an honor to meet him. As I turned away he asked if I practiced hard. I felt like saying, 'As hard as you,' but I was raised to be a gentleman and did not want to appear rude so I said, 'Yes, sir.' He said 'Good,

19TH HOLE

Player kisses the Claret Jug after winning his first Open Championship at Muirfield in 1959

then double it.' It took me some time to realize just how important that comment was and that is why I consider it my favorite story. Ben Hogan, one of the greatest golfers of all time, had just told me how he became the champion that he was: hard work and commitment. He dedicated himself to becoming a champion and when he reached that pinnacle he did not stop working, he worked harder. That is the true measure of greatness—the willingness to do whatever it takes and never giving up. I was taught that at an early age, but hearing that from Ben Hogan really made an impression on me."

HOLES IN ONE

Player, a nine-time major champion, has made twenty-seven holes in one in tournament competition. "I was playing in The Tradition, a major tournament on the Champions Tour at Desert Mountain Golf Course in Arizona with Jack Nicklaus and Arnold Palmer," Player said. "We came to the seventh hole, a par three. It was a double green, shared with the fifteenth hole, just like so many at St. Andrews . . . one big green. On the tee, which was highly elevated, with the wind behind us, I took a 6-iron and knocked the ball right into the cup! Then, we played around the rest of the way and came back to the same green, this time on the fifteenth hole, a par five. I managed to hole a wedge shot for my third [shot]. So, I had two eagles in the same round on the same green. Lyle Anderson, the owner and developer, kindly put a plaque on the back of the green saying, 'Gary Player: The only man to eagle the 7th and the 15th in the same round.' I'd say that was probably my most interesting hole in one shot and I've had twenty-seven in my career.

"Of course with my wife, Vivienne, having had two holes in one in the same round (which she keeps reminding me about), I have had this on my mind and have always wanted to achieve this myself," Player continued. "After my two eagles on this day, we came to the seventeenth hole, which is a par three. I hit my shot and the ball actually went right around the cup and stopped on the edge. I would have given anything to go to my wife and tell her that I also had two holes in one in the same round, but it just never worked out!"

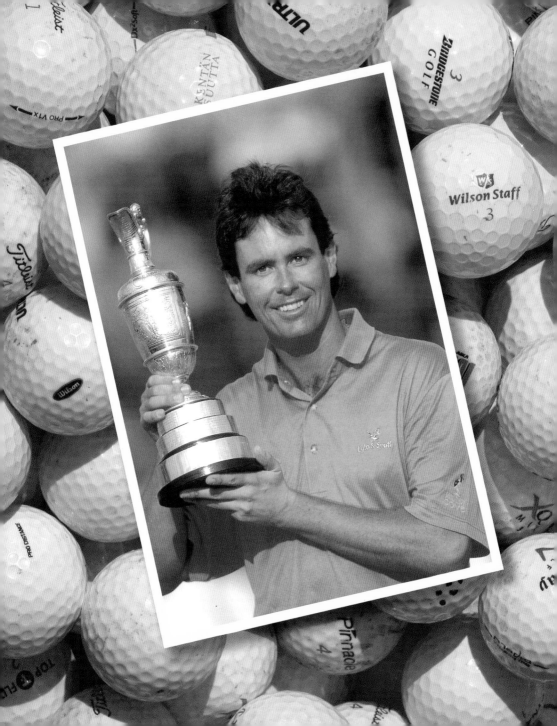

Ian Baker-Finch
Australia

FAVORITE DRINK

"I enjoy a cold beer after a round of golf," Baker-Finch said. "The funny thing with Australians [is] we always ask for a 'cold beer.' It almost doesn't matter what brand as long as it is very cold. I am also a wine lover, especially of the big California Cabernets and Australian Shiraz. A very popular drink that you see the ladies drinking in the golf clubs in Australia is a 'Shandy'—beer with 7-Up.

19TH HOLE

"The Medalist Golf Club in Hobe Sound, Florida, has a great locker room environment," Baker-Finch said. "It is one of my favorites, and they always have cold beer on tap.

"Another club where I spend a good deal of time because it is the closest to where I live is the Fox Club in Palm City, Florida. There is a big square bar in the middle of the clubhouse and all the members tee off at the same time so they return around the same time and you will always find twenty to forty people sitting around this giant square bar telling stories and enjoying a drink. It is really a fun, lively environment. The Old Sandwich Golf Club in Plymouth, Massachusetts, is a club built around the locker-room environment. When I am there I have breakfast, lunch, and dinner in the locker room. To me this is just perfect.

The 1991 Open Champion and I at Chelsea Piers Golf Club, New York City

"My most memorable celebration was after my Open Championship win in 1991 at the Royal Birkdale Golf Club in Southport, England. We had a party at the house and invited friends that were in town and the media to have dinner with us. My wife, Jennie, made spaghetti Bolognese and we had Foster's and great Australian red wine. It must have been about midnight when Jennie, my coach, Steve Bann, and I went back out to Birkdale and took the Claret Jug filled with great Australian wine and walked to the eighteenth green and just spent some time going over the round, drinking from the cup and taking photos. At some point the security came out to see what was going on. When they realized it was me they were very nice and I believe they even took some pictures for us. It was a really special moment."

Baker-Finch has had eight holes in one in competition and twelve more outside of competition. "I think it was around 1985 when I was playing the Japanese Tour," Baker-Finch said when asked about his most memorable ace. "I used a 3-iron and hit it two hundred and twelve yards for it to go in the hole. As a result I won a big bottle of scotch and prize money. I did not buy the clubhouse a round but the Aussie boys playing at the time and myself—we finished off the bottle of scotch that night!"

HOLES IN ONE

Bernhard Langer
Germany

Bernhard Langer was born in 1957 in Anhausen near Augsburg, Bavaria, Germany. He turned professional in 1976 and has won many events in Europe and the United States, among them the Masters in 1985 and 1993. He was the inaugural World Number 1 when the Official World Golf Rankings were introduced in 1986. He was elected to the World Golf Hall of Fame in 2001.

FAVORITE DRINK

"In Germany and especially Munich there is a drink that is very popular called the Radler," Langher said. "It is half Sprite and half beer. It is a refreshing drink and you do not get drunk. It is something I enjoy, especially in the summer. In England and other parts [of the world] they call this drink a Shandy."

19TH HOLE

The bar and restaurant at the Gut Lärchenhof Golf Club in Cologne, Germany, is Langer's favorite 19th hole. It is here that he hosted the last eleven years of the German Masters, later known as the Mercedes-Benz Championship. He finds the bar and restaurant at Gut Lärchenhof to be comfortable and cozy, making it easy to relax and enjoy post-golf moments.

The fabled Carnoustie Golf Links, where Langer captured the 2010 British Senior Open championship.

While Langer credits more than 100 tournament wins to his résumé, a recent celebration came after his win at the 2010 British Senior Open at Carnoustie Golf Links in Scotland. "I celebrated with my wife, brother, and his wife and some close friends drinking wine and enjoying the victory," Langer said.

HOLES IN ONE Langer has made fourteen holes in one. "The most memorable hole in one was probably in 1985 at the Australian Masters on the twelfth hole, he said. "I used an 8-iron to hit one hundred and fifty-five yards. I won a car and the tournament." When asked if he bought the clubhouse a round of drinks afterwards he laughed and noted there were about 20,000 spectators on-site so on that occasion he did not. He has more than once bought a round for 20–50 people after making a hole in one, though.

Lorena Ochoa
Mexico

Lorena Ochoa is from Guadalajara, Mexico, and was the number-one-ranked female golfer in the world for over three years, from April 2007 to May 2010. As the first Mexican golfer of either gender to be ranked number one in the world, she is considered the best Mexican golfer of all time.

An eleven-year-old Ochoa approached the professional Rafael Alarcon, 1979 winner of the Canadian Amateur Championship, as he worked on his game at Guadalajara Country Club, where her family lived near the 10th tee. She asked him if he would help her with her game. Alarcon asked her what her goal was. "She said she wanted to be the best player in the world."

FAVORITE DRINK

"Horchata is one of my favorite drinks," Ochoa said. Horchata is a tan, usually milky-looking drink that is made of rice, sometimes with vanilla and always with cinnamon. "When I am playing golf I drink a mix of Gatorade powder with water. Tequila is very popular in my country and it is meant to be sipped with a meal. That is how it is used in Mexico very often.

19TH HOLE   "Guadalajara Country Club, where I grew up playing, is my favorite place to relax," Ochoa said. "The terrace is open and looks out onto the eighteenth green and the putting area. I have always enjoyed having lunch there and spending time with friends and family. When I was growing up and practicing I could hear the people talking while they were having lunch and could tell who was there from the voices. I did not even have to look up. I have very fond memories [of that club]. It is a beautiful place and very special."

HOLES IN ONE   Ochoa has made nine holes in one but only one during tournament play. "It was a big surprise because there were bunkers in the way so I could not see where the ball went," Ochoa said. "I just heard people screaming and jumping up and down. I did not even get to see it go in. I just picked it out of the cup when I got to the green.

"I did not buy the clubhouse a round as it was during tournament play. My coach, Rafael Alarcon, made a hole in one while we were practicing and he invited us to lunch at the Guadalajara Country Club. It is a very special time when someone makes a hole in one. I think it is good reason for a player to celebrate."

Lee Westwood
England

For twenty-two weeks in 2010, Lee Westwood was the number-one-ranked golfer in the world. Noted for his consistency, he is one of the few golfers who has won tournaments on every major continent. He was the runner-up at both the 2010 Masters and Open Championship in 2010.

FAVORITE DRINK

"The drinks I enjoy are a sea breeze (vodka, cranberry, and grapefruit), especially when I am on the beach," Westwood said. "Also a vodka tonic, rose wine, and champagne. After a win, champagne is best. In England we are known for tea and I definitely drink tea two to three times a day when I am home in England. I don't usually drink tea when I am away on the road, only when I am home. It tastes different here.

19TH HOLE

"An interesting story about a bar or 19th hole came during the 1996 Volvo Scandinavian Masters," Westwood said. "Saturday night after play Stuart Cage, my good friend and best man at my wedding, and I went into the pub to get a beer before going to bed. They would not serve us as they thought we looked too young. The next

day I ended up winning the tournament in a playoff and went back to the bar. This time I had no problem getting in or [getting] a drink.

"I [also] have a very fond memory of the 1998 Bay Hill Invitational—the year Ernie Els won. I remember being in the locker room with my caddy, Ernie Els, his caddy, Arnold Palmer, and Chubby Chandler. We all just sat and talked for a while over drinks. It was a very nice time.

"Another great moment was the time we celebrated after I won the Dubai World Championship," Westwood continued. "[At] the Jumeirah Hotel Chubby Chandler and friends all got together and organized a great party on the beach. It was quite a celebration. We may have had a Shandy or two."

TWO GOOD ROUNDS

Westwood estimates that he has made around a dozen holes in one. "My most memorable is probably my first one when I was thirteen years old. It was on the 3rd hole of the Worksop Golf Club in Worksop, UK," Westwood said. "I used a driver and hit it one hundred and eighty-five yards. My dad was with me and when we went back to the clubhouse he bought a bottle of whiskey for the people at the bar. I have [also] bought a round for the clubhouse in the past when I was in Portugal."

HOLES IN ONE

LEE WESTWOOD

Stuart Appleby
Australia

Stuart Appleby's favorite drink is beer. "I usually enjoy a beer from Australia," Appleby said. "Victorian Bitter—VB—or Carlton Draft, and you can get them at most bottle shops in Australia. However, the beers are very regional. Crown Lager is a premium beer that I also enjoy. The Australian embassy in Washington, DC, would sometimes have the Australian beers, and Robert Allenby and I once brought some down to Florida.

"I have a wine cellar and some of the wines are fourteen years old," he continued. "I really enjoy a nice Australian wine as well. For me they are a simple connection to home. I have four children now so I am not out too much. Once in a while I enjoy a vodka and red bull, but I have to give it the utmost respect.

"As a kid growing up I probably had hundreds of 'lemon squash' (a sparkling lemon drink). I would come back to the clubhouse after a round at my home course, Cohuna Golf Club (in the Murray River region of Victoria, Australia), and sit with my friends. We would run through hypothetical scenarios of playing in tournaments. We would role-play about beating the great golfers. Greg Norman was a big influence in Australia and we would role-play going head to head at the Masters with Greg or we would emulate

FAVORITE DRINK

famous golfers' swings and golf mannerisms. Now, as an accomplished golfer, I guess if I had a wishful golf dream it would be winning [The Open Championship] at St. Andrews in 2015 and sitting in the clubhouse with all my friends and after, when everyone had gone, I would walk up eighteen late at night with a few good friends and the trophy in hand. I know 'Finchy' (Ian Baker-Finch) did that after he won The Open."

HOLES IN ONE Appleby has made four holes in one. "On the first day of a tournament I was one of the first groups out and I was on the second hole and I hit right into the sun," Appleby said when asked about his most memorable ace. "I walked behind the green looking for the ball and there were two guys sitting there. When I asked them if they had seen the ball they replied, 'Yeah it went in the hole.' They did not even clap or get out of their seats.

"The other holes in one [I made] were when I was an amateur and I did not have money to buy the clubhouse a round. My dad was a farmer and he never wasted a minute. He was up early milking cows and would drive me from one tournament to another four and [a] half hours. I credit my work ethic as a player to that. I have always been prudent and focused before and now that I have kids."

TWO GOOD ROUNDS

Mr. 59

In the entire history of the PGA Tour, which dates back to 1916, only five players have shot a 59 in tournament competition. So what did "Mr. 59" do to celebrate his low score at Greenbrier Classic in West Virginia in 2010? "I had a few beers with the family," Appleby said.

Paul Goydos, who did it July 8 at the John Deere Classic, along with David Duval (1999 Bob Hope), Chip Beck (1991 Las Vegas Invitational), and the original Mr. 59, Al Geiberger (1977 Memphis Classic), are the only other tour players to accomplish the feat.

Appleby's historic scorecard

Stuart Appleby's winning 59

	1	2	3	4	5	6	7	8	9	OUT	10	11	12	13	14	15	16	17	18	IN	TOT
Par	4	4	3	4	4	4	4	3	4	34	4	4	5	4	4	3	4	5	3	36	70
Round 4	4	③	3	③	③	③	③	3	③	28	4	4	③	4	4	3	③	④	②	31	59

Me and Appleby at the 2011 Tavistock Cup

Michael Campbell
New Zealand

"In New Zealand white wines are quite popular," said Campbell, the 2005 U.S. Open champion. "I like a Sauvignon Blanc or a chardonnay and occasionally a beer. Beer is also quite popular in New Zealand. After I play a round of golf I enjoy relaxing in the clubhouse with a Pinot by Herzog. This is my favorite red.

"My favorite clubhouse spot is the 'Tiger Room' at the Kauri Cliffs in Matauri Bay, New Zealand," Campbell said. "The name Tiger Room has nothing to do with Tiger Woods. The owner of Kauri Cliffs is Julian Robertson, the former American hedge fund manager. Robertson founded the investment firm Tiger Management Corp., one of the earliest hedge funds. The room is named after the fund. The views from the golf course and entire complex are magnificent. It is an unbelievably beautiful place. I enjoy sitting in the Tiger Room with a glass of Hans Herzog Pinot Noir after a round of golf.

Campbell with famed hedge fund manager Julian Robertson

"I grew up playing on a nine-hole course called Tatahi Golf Club that was in a farm area," Campbell continued. "There were fences around the greens to keep the sheep

MICHAEL CAMPBELL

out. It has changed over the years but it is still a nine-hole course. My dad used to take me to the golf course. I remember it was five dollars for a round of golf. Every Sunday he would ask me if I wanted to go and caddy for him. He would pay me with a strawberry milkshake and a meat pie. I thought that was the greatest thing. It was not cool in the early eighties to play golf. At the time I was fourteen and no one played or watched golf—it was for the upper class and wealthy. We had a sports activity day for school where they took us to a golf course and my friends did not know I had already been playing for five years. I was a five handicap at the time and when we got to the range I was hitting them straight and far while everyone was learning to grip the club. They were surprised.

"A really nice memory I have is after my U.S. Open win at Pinehurst in 2005. After I had finished all the media stuff a bunch of us went over to the clubhouse bar at the Pine Needles hotel where I was staying, which is also a golf course. So this would probably be my best 19th hole moment. I celebrated with two hundred people. We were in the lobby and the bar called the 'Rough Lounge.' I drank champagne out of the trophy cup and had a great time. I remember waking up the next morning and seeing the trophy on the nightstand and thinking, *Is this a dream or is it real?*

"When I returned to New Zealand after my U.S. Open win there was a parade. My parents were on floats and one hundred and ten thousand people lined the streets of Wellington. I realized what a huge impact my win had made on people and it was an incredible feeling. It was the second most attended parade. The first was [for] the Beatles."

Campbell holding the US Open Trophy after his 2005 victory

Campbell has made two holes in one. "The first was when I was fifteen years old," he said. "I was playing in a practice round and I used a 7-iron on the seventeenth hole of a course in New Zealand. I was too young to buy drinks. I must have had a soft drink in the clubhouse."

HOLES IN ONE

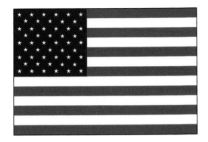

Jim Furyk
United States

"What I drink depends on the occasion," Furyk, the 2003 U.S. Open champion, said. "When I am playing golf I drink a lot of water. I enjoy a cold beer after a round and Johnnie Walker Gold on ice is refreshing and what I really enjoy in the evening. I do enjoy a cocktail now and again and I like a scotch neat, Johnnie Walker Black.

FAVORITE DRINK

"I am sure when you get a bunch of golfers together in a 19th hole environment, you can get some exaggerated stories," Furyk said. "My best 19th hole memory was when I was sixteen. I was able to join Meadia Heights Golf Club in Lancaster County, Pennsylvania, as a junior member. In 1986, two of my friends and I were in the 19th hole clubhouse bar watching the Masters on Sunday. Jack Nicklaus was making his charge and as the final round progressed the bar started to fill up. We had been there since the start of the coverage and we realized how lucky we were to still be in the bar area and watching as Jack won. Now that I know Jack it is even more special, also considering that it was the last time he won the Masters."

19TH HOLE

Furyk has made eleven holes in one. "I have two favorite hole-in-one stories," he said. "The first time I ever made a hole in one I was twelve years old and playing with my dad in Lancaster, Pennsylva-

HOLES IN ONE

nia. It was getting dark as we approached the eighteenth hole and I used a 3-iron on the par 3. The other is in 2010 at the Masters during the par 3 tournament on Wednesday. I had my son, Tanner, and daughter, Cali, caddying for me. I almost got a hole in one on the second hole and the kids were very excited. I explained to them since it is a par 3 I was trying to make a hole in one on every hole. I told Cali that I did not want to make it on the nineth hole, because that was the hole where she would get to putt. Sure enough I made a hole in one on the ninth. After we took the ball out we dropped the ball on the green so Cali still got to putt. It was a great moment."

CLUBHOUSE DRINK

Furyk found himself in an interesting situation in 2010 at the Barclays, when he was disqualified from the tournament because he missed his 7:30 AM pro-am tee time on Wednesday, the day before the tournament began. Furyk, ranked no. three in the FedEx Cup standings at the time, overslept after his cell-phone alarm clock lost power overnight. He awoke at 7:23 AM and rushed to Ridgewood Country Club, the site of the first of four playoff events that each carried a $7.5 million purse. The pro-am began at 7:30 AM with a shotgun start, but Furyk could not get to his starting hole—the 11th—in time after arriving to the course at 7:35 AM.

Jim squelched any suspicion that his appearance at a Johnnie Walker tasting and meet and greet at Chelsea Piers the night before had anything to do with his lateness. "It was a great event and I wish I was tasting more that night," he said. "But I got there early and met with the master taster at the event and tried a few things and then went to a simulator and played with guests all night where they had to try to beat me. It was a very nice event and I was home early. In the end I won the FedEx Cup so it all worked out."

Angel Cabrera
Argentina

FAVORITE DRINK

"Red wine is my favorite drink," Cabrera said. "In Argentina Malbec is very popular and it is what I enjoy the most. *Mate cocido* is an herb-like tea that is also very famous in Argentina. People drink it like tea and often in a gourd with a special straw called a *bomba/bombilla*. I do enjoy drinking mate but I prefer it in a tea cup not in the gourd."

Mate is the national drink in Argentina and the most common preparation involves a careful arrangement of the yerba within the gourd before adding hot water. Drinking yerba mate is considered to be more than just good for the body; it's also considered to be good for the soul. Drinking it can be a form of meditation or reflection, allowing the goodness to infuse into the body while stimulating and resting the mind.

A gourd filled with mate

19TH HOLE

"My favorite spot to relax is [on] the terrace of the Cordoba Golf Club in the late afternoon, when it is shady," Cabrera said. "This is my home course, the course where I grew up playing and have gone my whole life. The best place is the terrace. You can see the whole golf course."

Cordoba Golf Club is the home course of two great golfers, "El Pato," Angel Cabrera, and "El Gato," Eduardo Romero. In 2007 Cabrera became the first Argentine player to win the U.S. Open and the second to win a major, joining Roberto De Vicenzo, who won the British Open in 1967 at Royal Liverpool. Cabrera is also the first Argentine to win the Masters.

"Two very special moments for me are my 2007 U.S. Open win at Oakmont and my 2009 win at the Masters," Cabrera said. "Maybe this is not necessarily a nineteenth hole celebration directly after a win, but a very special event for me was hosting the Champions Dinner at the Masters. This is a really nice tradition they have at Augusta National for the Masters, where the returning Masters champion selects the Champions Dinner menu." As is tradition, Cabrera got to choose the menu for the 2010 Masters' Champions Dinner held Tuesday night of Masters week.

"We had a great *Asado de Argentina,* an Argentine beef dinner with wines from Argentina," Cabrera said. *Asado* is a term used both for a range of barbecue techniques and the social event of having or attending a barbecue in Argentina. An asado usually consists of beef alongside various other meats, which are cooked on a grill, called a *parrilla,* or open fire. It is considered a traditional dish in Argentina. Usually the asado will begin by igniting the coal. The coal will usually be made of native trees, avoiding pines and eucalyptus that have strong-smelling resins. In more sophisticated asados, the coal would be of a specific tree or made on the coal of recently burned wood. The meat is not marinated. Rather, it receives its flavor from the coals.

Cabrera has made twenty-two holes in one since turning pro. "Two
very memorable holes in one were the ones I had at Valderrama
San Roque, Spain, and one at The K Club—the Kildare Hotel and
Country Club, Kildare, Ireland," Cabrera said. When asked if he
bought the clubhouse a round afterwards, he laughed and said,
"Luckily there was no one there" since it was a tournament. "When
I have gotten a hole in one during tournaments usually the four-
some I am with will have a beer afterwards."

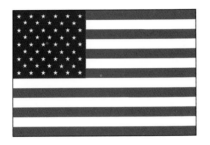

Christina Kim
United States

Christina Kim's parents are South Korean but she was born and raised in San Jose, California. Kim is well known and loved for her animated and vocal style of play, flamboyant dress, and outgoing personality.

"I love to drink, period!" Kim joked. "Tanqueray and tonic, Grey Goose and Red Bull, and Jägerbombs. (The Jägerbomb is a bomb shot cocktail that is mixed by dropping a shot of Jägermeister into a glass of Red Bull). "When I am feeling like a nerdy wine drinker I will have a Sauvignon Blanc. I tried Mike Weir's red wine when I was in Canada and I liked it. I also enjoy a Shirley Temple when I am not drinking alcohol. It is a fun drink.

FAVORITE DRINK

"I like the Eye Bar at PGA National," Kim said. "A really special place is the Old Palm Golf Club in Palm Beach Gardens, because they have a 19th hole—an extra hole that is a one hundred-yard island green about the size of a coffee table that was built for settling wagers.

19TH HOLE

"Some of the best times I have had with the other women on the LPGA were at the Solheim Cup," Kim continued. "It is always

Kim enjoying a laugh with me and golf writer Alan Shipnuck, who collaborated with Christina on her book, Swinging from My Heels

good fun. It is like a sorority. Whatever happens at Solheim Cup stays at Solheim Cup.

"One of the best times was after the HSBC Women's Champions in Singapore. Thirty of us went out to the Pump Room, a very fun place that has great live cover bands."

HOLES IN ONE   Kim has made eight holes in one in her life. "The best ace was in 2006 at the Ginn Club and Resort Open," Kim said. "I was on the eleventh hole and I hit a 9-iron one hundred and thirty-four yards. I was in the final group and I jumped four feet in the air. I did not buy the clubhouse drinks after the hole in one because it was during a tournament. However I have bought the boys a round. I was out with Lee Westwood and a few other guys. Chubby Chandler's boys. We all have the same management team, ISM, so I did buy them a round last time I saw them."

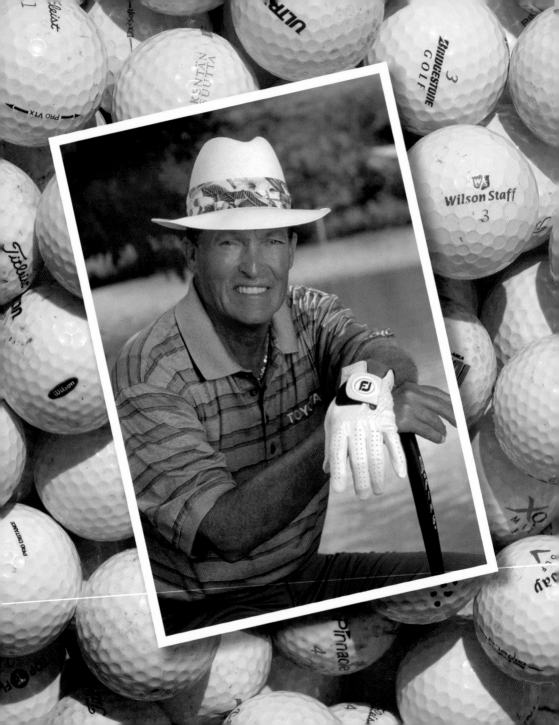

Chi-Chi Rodriguez
Puerto Rico

"When having a cocktail my drink is Johnnie Walker Blue, some-times a mimosa or a rum and Coke or *Cuba Libre*, as we call it," said Rodriguez. "I still enjoy an occasional root beer and ginger ale.

FAVORITE DRINK

"I really enjoy going to a few golf clubs in Puerto Rico," Rodriguez said. "The Wyndham Rio Mar Beach Resort and Golf Club and The Plantation Club at Dorado Beach in Dorado, Puerto Rico. Both are family oriented, relaxed and have excellent service.

19TH HOLE

"This is interesting because I have done everything on a golf course. I have been a starter, picked range balls, [been an] assistant pro and teaching pro, and also caddied. It wasn't until I was twenty-three years old that I was able to go into the clubhouse because I was a caddy and at the time we were not allowed in.

"I remember my caddy [once] saying after a win, 'They are warming up the champagne.' It was funny at the time. I also re-member Lee Trevino saying, 'We used to be waiters in places like this and now we are celebrating.' After winning [a tournament] in Panama one time I drank a little too much and got up and sang most of the night. One of my favorite songs I sing is 'Bésame Bés-ame Mucho.'"

HOLES IN ONE Rodriguez claims to have made thirty-seven holes in one. "At one point I was number one in the world with the most holes in one," he said. "The first hole in one was when I was ten years old. I used a 7-iron and hit it one hundred and five yards. I played with an amateur that missed a hole in one by three strokes."

Rodriguez's most significant ace came "during a tournament for my foundation (The Chi-Chi Rodríguez Youth Foundation, an afterschool program at the Glen Oaks Golf Course in Clearwater, Florida) on a par three course. I had five hundred people following me and I told them I was going to hit a hole in one. I hit the tree and it shot off the tree and to the back then in the hole.

"I make all my hole in ones on Mondays when no one is around so I do not have to buy drinks."

TWO GOOD ROUNDS

The Plantation Club at Dorado Beach

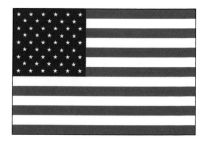

Jack Nicklaus
United States

"Most of the time, I drink water," Nicklaus, the eighteen-time major champion, said. "But occasionally, if I am in a social setting, I might have cranberry juice and iced tea—decaf iced tea, that is. And if I am attending an evening function, I might enjoy a glass of red wine."

    Nicklaus's decision to launch a Jack Nicklaus wine label with Bill Terlato came about as a result of Jack's interest in collecting wines over the years. Nicklaus and his sons, Jack II and Gary, visited Terlato-owned vineyards in California to meet with founder Anthony Terlato and his sons, Bill and John. They toured the Terlato-owned wineries, and what emerged was a new friendship and two fabulous new wines.

    The line of Jack Nicklaus Wines includes a Cabernet Sauvignon and a Private Reserve—both from the 2007 vintage. The Cabernet is full-bodied and rich, with intense flavor; the Private Reserve incorporates both Bordeaux grapes and Syrah.

FAVORITE DRINK

"If I had a favorite story, it might be the wig story, with Arnold Palmer in Palm Springs," Nicklaus said. "That might be one story

19TH HOLE

The Nicklaus and Terlato families at the Terlato family vineyard

more people have enjoyed than any I can recall. Back in the 1960s and '70s, it was common for clubs to hold jam sessions after tournament play. Many times these would be in the clubhouse of the host venue. At the Bob Hope in Palm Springs, they frequently had these sessions after the tournament, which was a lot of fun. All the golfers, musicians, and celebrities would gather and just jam. People would just get up and sing. There was music going all the time and people were dancing. It's kind of like what Vince Gill does each year at his charity tournament. Well, one year in Palm Springs—I believe it was 1972—I remember Arnold and I were at this one particular jam session. We both got up to go to the bathroom, and on our way back, we accidentally brushed up against this lady with a wig on. I'm not sure if it was Arnold or me who brushed her, but we knocked her wig off. One of us picked it up and put it on the other's head and we went straight to the dance floor and started dancing. The poor girl had to have been mortified. Out of that came this famous photo of me wearing the wig while we were dancing.

TWO GOOD ROUNDS

Well, I am not sure who was wearing the wig when we were dancing. I think one of us put it on and then we traded. So there might
be several photos out there.

"Those jam sessions were always a lot of fun. We used to
do it at a lot of places, like the Crosby and the Hope. And many of
those took place in the clubhouse. Those are the kind of things we
used to do.

"I guess you could say I don't have a special place, but I have
a lot of special memories from a lot of places where we played
tournaments and then gathered afterwards. Sometimes it was just
the guys getting together and sometimes you would bring your
wife. It was just good fun. Those days reflected the true social
nature of golf."

*The infamous 1972
wig photo. Compli-
ments of* The Ameri-
can Golfer.

Vijay Singh
Fiji

"When I finish playing or am relaxing my favorite drink is a margarita," Singh said. I also drink Fiji water, which is really from Fiji. Kava is the traditional drink in Fiji. It is a little too sweet for me. " Kava is an age-old herbal drink that was the beverage of choice for the royal families of the South Pacific. This traditional drink still plays a key role in Fijian societies where it is drank in ceremonies meant to honor visitors, unite participants, and validate social identities. Kava is made from the bare root of a pepper tree, pounded into a fine powder and then mixed with fresh water.

FAVORITE DRINK

"I really enjoy the clubhouse and the locker room at the TPC Players Club in Ponte Vedra, Florida," Singh said. "It is so familiar and comfortable for me. This is my home course, so this is where I can relax the best."

19TH HOLE

Singh estimates that he has made approximately ten to fifteen holes in one. His most memorable came on the fourteenth hole at the Valhalla Golf Club in Louisville, Kentucky, from two hundred and twenty yards. "I never made a hole in one in Fiji," Singh said. "Otherwise I would have bought the clubhouse a round of drinks."

HOLES IN ONE

Mike Weir
Canada

In 2003, Mike Weir won the Masters, making him the first Canadian male ever to win a major championship. Weir also became only the second left-handed golfer to win any of the four majors, the other being Bob Charles, who won the British Open forty years earlier.

While working at Huron Oaks, he met Jack Nicklaus at age eleven, when the golf legend came to the club to play an exhibition. This meeting set the stage for a pivotal moment in Weir's career.

Weir gave up hockey in his early teenage years when he realized he would not grow past average size and that golf was his best sport. However, he had received advice that he might be an even better golfer if he switched to playing right-handed. In 1984, Weir decided to write Nicklaus for advice as to whether to make the switch. Nicklaus quickly wrote back and told Weir, "If you are a good player left-handed, don't change anything—especially if that feels natural to you." He never thought of switching to right-handed play again, and still keeps the letter framed in his home.

"Most times after golf or on a hot summer day I enjoy a beer—Canadian beer, usually Molson Canadian," Weir said. Mike and his family launched Mike Weir Estate Winery in 2005. Mike Weir Wine is made in the Niagara Region of Canada. The wine creation is an-

FAVORITE DRINK

other example of his love for his home country. "I can promise you that I'll bring the same passion and commitment to quality wine as I have to my golf career and I hope you join me in that journey," Weir said. Weir Wines produces a Cabernet Merlot, Pinot Noir, Sauvignon Blanc, and a chardonnay. The chardonnay has won awards and is Mike's personal favorite.

19TH HOLE   Weir's top three 19th holes begin with the Huron Oaks Golf Course in Ontario where he grew up playing."The french fries with gravy [at Huron Oaks] are the best," Weir says, "which is how Canadians like their french fries. The Champions locker room at Augusta National is [also] a favorite for its simple but fantastic food, and the Glenwild Golf Course in Park City, Utah's locker grill room is another great place."

Weir has made eight holes in one. "The first hole in one when I was a junior is my most memorable," he said. "I used a 3-iron and it was on the eighth hole of the Chedoke Golf Club in Hamilton, Ontario. I was a junior so I did not buy the clubhouse a round. However another time when I made a hole in one it was just my wife and I and I did buy her a drink. When I have won tournaments I usually go down to the caddy trailer that day and buy all the caddies lunch."

HOLES IN ONE

Ryuji Imada
Japan

Ryuji Imada (今田竜二) was born in Mihara, Hiroshima, Japan. He came to the United States when he was fourteen to attend a Tampa golf academy for Asian players. To date he has three professional victories playing on the Nationwide and PGA Tours.

"There are a few drinks that are popular and well known from Japan," Imada said. "Sake, which many people know, is more of a winter drink. Shōchū is also very popular. This is a distilled potato drink. There are two well-known beers that people drink in Japan but that can also be found in the USA and other places. The two most popular beers are Asahi and Kirin. "I do not drink alcohol, so I guess what I drink most is apple juice and Perrier."

FAVORITE DRINK

Bottles of shōchū

19TH HOLE Avila Country Club in Tampa is Imada's home course and where he feels most comfortable in the clubhouse. "I can chit-chat with my buddies and play cards and have dinner [there]," he said.

HOLES IN ONE Imada has made four holes in one. "I remember making a hole in one during a school match when I was seventeen years old in Chamberlain Tampa Babe Zaharias High School," he said. "It was on the eighth hole and I used a 7-iron."

Hole-In-One Insurance?

"An interesting thing about Japan is they have national insurance you can take out for holes in one," Imada said. "It is two thousand dollars to five thousand dollars a year for insurance. It can get crazy if you get a hole in one because there it is customary to have something made like towels and balls printed announcing your hole in one and that you give it to everyone that is a member of the club. This can get very costly, so they have insurance."

TWO GOOD ROUNDS

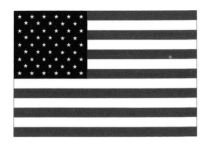

Natalie Gulbis
United States

"Michelob Ultra and Michelob Amber are my favorite drinks," Gulbis said. "For me it is a natural fit as growing up in an American sports family Budweiser was always around.

FAVORITE DRINK

"I grew up playing at Whitney Oaks Golf Course in Sacramento, California, and I have very fond memories of going into the club-house after playing golf and playing liar's dice," Gulbis said. "It is a cup dice game. When I go home now it is a great feeling because I just pick up where I left off. After practicing and playing golf I will go in the clubhouse, have a beer and sit around with family and friends telling stories and playing liar's dice. My dad worked the graveyard shift in law enforcement and he would play golf during the day. I used to tag along and I remember him having a beer at the 19th hole.

19TH HOLE

"In 2007 I won my first tournament in France at the Evian Masters and the next tournament was in England, so I had to go straight to England. When I got home, Mich-

On the red carpet at the 2009 ESPY Awards in Los Angeles

NATALIE GULBIS

elob Ultra had sent ice chests to my home course and filled them with beer and they were on every hole of my home course.

"I like to throw parties at my homes in Las Vegas and Sacramento and enjoy getting people together for a celebration."

HOLES IN ONE

Gulbis has made thirteen holes in one. "The most significant was at an LPGA event, The Michelob ULTRA Open at Kingsmill Resort and Spa in Virginia," Gulbis said. "It was on the thirteenth hole; I used an 8-iron and hit it one hundred and fifty yards. There was a very big gallery and the whole place exploded. It was a great feeling.

"I remember once buying the clubhouse a round of drinks at my home course in Sacramento. You don't need any big event or reason to drink a beer. After ten months on the road I enjoy coming home and meeting up with friends and family. That is reason enough."

A neon 19th hole advertisement for Michelob, Gulbis's favorite beer.

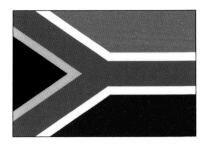

Ernie Els
South Africa

"Wine is my favorite drink," Els said. "So much so I guess that I started my own winery. We now have six labels."

FAVORITE DRINK

A total of six wines are now housed under the Ernie Els Wines portfolio. The Ernie Els Signature is the flagship wine. In addition there is the Ernie Els Proprietor's Blend, the Big Easy, the Ernie Els Proprietor's Syrah, the Ernie Els Cabernet Sauvignon, and the Ernie Els Merlot.

The Signature Blend wine is made up of five Bordeaux varieties to reflect the unique diversity of the Stellenbosch. This wine, made by cellar master Louis Strydom, is Ernie Els and Jean Engelbrecht's vision to produce an exceptional wine, reflecting their respective commitment to quality. The different clones of Cabernet Sauvignon, Cabernet Franc, Merlot, Malbec, and Petit Verdot are kept separate (micro-vinified) throughout vinification.

Enjoying a glass of Els' Big Easy wine at the IGTM banquet in Valencia, Spain

The Big Easy Restaurant and Wine Bar in Stellenbosch is in the heart of wine country in South Africa. This is also a well-known student town.

"We bought a historic house, restored it, and created the restaurant and wine bar," Els said. The building was built in 1798 by the first reverend of Stellenbosch

ERNIE ELS

91

and is a combination of Cape Dutch, Georgian, and Victorian architecture.

The building features memorabilia and photos through the years of "The Big Easy" doing what he does best—golf. Two of the dining rooms are named "The Golf Estate room" and "The Wine Estate room" after two of Ernie's favorite interests.

19TH HOLE "On a night out after a tournament win I buy most of the drinks," Els said. "The most memorable celebration was after my tournament win in 2002, The Open Championship at Muirfield Golf Links in Scotland. It was at the Jigger Inn, next to the Old Course Hotel at St. Andrews. Nick Price got a bunch of friends together and told my wife, Liezl, to bring me there and when I walked in he drenched me in champagne. I think we left around 2 AM.

"My 1998 win at Bay Hill is [also] very memorable just because after I had won I sat in the locker room at Bay Hill with Arnold Palmer and Lee Westwood and we had drinks and talked golf.

"The Burma Bar at Wentworth is also a great spot. I may

have started celebrating at breakfast." Els, who won seven World Match Play titles on the course, has every right to celebrate. Els also has a home on the Wentworth Estate southwest of London, and redesigned the West Course at Wentworth in 2005 when he did not play because of a knee injury. As Angel Cabrera put it after losing to Els at Wentworth in 2007, "Ernie is the king of Wentworth."

Els has made nine holes in one. "I never win anything like a car," Els said. "The most I have won is a bottle of champagne.

"My most memorable [hole in one] was during the 1997 PGA Championship at Winged Foot, when I got a hole in one on the tenth hole using a 6-iron.

"The best one was in the 2004 British Open, on the famous 'Postage Stamp,' the par-three eighth hole at Royal Troon. There are grandstands all around that green so the cheer from the crowd was huge. That was very special. The ball bounced twice left of the flagstick, spun wickedly toward the hole, and dropped in from the backside."

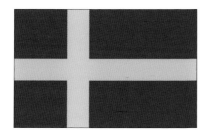

Jesper Parnevik
Sweden

"Both vodka and schnapps are very popular in Sweden," Parnevik said. "People drink it at the holidays and in the summer. Something quite popular in Sweden is that people often sing a song before they do the shot. Everyone knows these songs—it is something traditional and common. I myself like an ice-cold Coke after a round of golf and if I am relaxing at the grill room I enjoy a beer or red wine.

FAVORITE DRINK

"My favorite clubhouse would be La Manga in Alicante, Spain," Parnevik said. "I went [there] every year with my parents as a child, and that is where I won the European tour school to get on tour.

19TH HOLE

"A great celebration for me was in 2002 after we, the Europeans, won the Ryder Cup held at Belfry. I had two entertainers from Sweden come and perform in the bar. Everyone was dancing on the tables, some people missed their flights. Some of the Americans joined in as well. It was a really great time.

"How I started playing golf is our family went to Spain for vacation and my parents liked to play golf. I would go with my dad as a kid—I was around thirteen—

and I used to play golf because he would promise me a Coke and a Croque-monsieur (grilled ham and cheese sandwich) after the round. This was a big thing then. Coke was not everywhere like it is now. Golf was not popular in Sweden. As a matter of fact I was the only kid in my town and school to play golf. I brought a golf club and a golf ball to school for show-and-tell one time. So you can imagine at thirteen it was not cool to golf. I really went and played with my dad for the Coke and the Croque-monsieur.

HOLES IN ONE
"I made a hole in one during the 1994–1995 World Cup when it was held in China at Mission Hills," Parnevik said. "I was playing with Freddy Davis and as a result I won free Heineken for one year. So I guess you can say instead of buying the clubhouse a round I bought a lot of our friends rounds for a year! Every time we would have a party we would order the Heineken.

"I was playing with my caddy, Lance, and Dan Quinn and another friend on a course in Florida near my house. A strange hole in one story is that four of us went to play golf and I made a hole in one on the fourteenth hole with my 7-iron. The next week the four of us played again and I made a hole in one on the exact same hole with the same club. Two weeks in a row, two holes in one, on the same hole using the same club."

COURTESY OF *Kyle Auclair*,
TourPlayers.com

Edoardo Molinari
Italy

"One of the most famous drinks from my country is cappuccino," Molinari said. "Cappuccino is a typical Italian drink, made of espresso coffee, hot milk, and steamed-milk froth. It is great to have a cappuccino after a round of golf in cold winter weather. When I come back in the clubhouse feeling a little bit cold," Molinari continued, "I am really looking forward to have a nice hot cappuccino with a slice of cake or a croissant."

FAVORITE DRINK

Cappuccino

19TH HOLE "My favorite grill room is definitely the bar room at Circolo Golf Torino, my home club," Molinari said. "Circolo Golf Torino–La Mandria in Fiano, Italy. Ten years after Italy became a republic in 1946, Circolo Golf Torino moved to the Parco Regionale La Mandria, the old hunting estate of the former ruling House of Savoy.

"In Italy you can stay in the bar even when you are not eighteen years old yet, but you cannot buy drinks," Molinari said. "Since I was a child I've spent a lot of time in the clubhouse there and even though I am not too keen on drinking, I've spent a lot of time sitting there in the bar with my friends after having played a tight game with them. My best friend is a great storyteller, and we still play golf together these days and we always go in the bar after our round to have a laugh."

Molinari has made three holes in one. "The first one was at Sestriere Golf Club, a small golf club up in the mountains near Turin," he said. "I was fourteen years old and I was too young to buy drinks, so I got away with that one! I did not buy the clubhouse a round."

Making History

The undisputed highlight of Molinari's amateur career came in 2005, when he became the first Italian and the first Continental European to win the U.S. Amateur. He claimed the title by holing a 25-foot birdie putt on the 33rd hole to win 4 & 3 over American Dillon Dougherty. As a result of that victory, Molinari qualified to play in the 2006 Masters, U.S. Open, and The Open Championship.

Both Edoardo and his brother Francisco Molinari competed as part of the 2010 European Ryder Cup team, becoming the first set of brothers to compete together in a Ryder Cup side since Bernard and Geoffry Hunt played for the Great Britain and Ireland side in the 1963 edition of the biennial team competition.

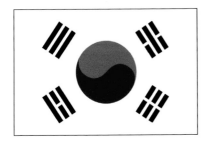

K. J. Choi
South Korea

"A well-known traditional drink from Korea that people have been drinking from long time ago is *makgeolli* and *sikhye*," Choi said. *makgeolli*, also known as *makuly (takju)*, is an alcoholic beverage native to Korea. It is made from rice (referred to in English as "Korean rice wine") which gives it a milky, off-white color, and sweetness. It is made by fermenting a mixture of boiled rice and water, and is about 6.5–7% alcohol by volume. It was originally quite popular among farmers, earning it the name *nongju* (˙ ˙ / 農酒), which means "farmer liquor." However, it has recently started to become more popular in cities, especially with the younger generations.

A bowl of makgeolli

Sikhye (also spelled *shikhye* or *shikeh*; also occasionally termed *dansul* or *gamju*) is a traditional sweet Korean rice beverage, usually served as a dessert. In addition to its liquid ingredients, *sikhye* also contains grains of cooked rice, and in some cases pine nuts. *Sikhye* is made by pouring malt water onto cooked rice. The malt water steeps in the rice at typically 150 degrees Fahrenheit until grains of rice appear on the surface. The liquid is then carefully poured out, leaving the rougher parts, and boiled with sugar. Ginger or jujube is often added for additional flavor. It is served chilled.

19TH HOLE "My favorite grill room is The Club at the Vaquero Country Club in Westlake, Texas, which is the golf course where I currently live and practice," Choi said. "The chef there makes great food and my favorites on the menu are the grilled sea bass and the lamb chop. The chef makes his special sauces which have a sweet yet distinct flavor. I go there often for lunch with family or when I have guests."

HOLES IN ONE "My first hole in one came in 2005 during the HP Classic in New Orleans at English Turn," Choi said. "It was on the par-three twelfth hole, which played one hundred and fifty-six yards from the tee on that day. I had back wind, with the pin placed on the front left of the green. The hole played downwards but sloping up as you walked up to the green. I hit a 9-iron to the front of the green which bounced twice and disappeared into the hole. I remember high-fiving my playing partners. Unfortunately for them, it was during a tournament so they missed out on getting a free round of beer from me!"

Fuzzy Zoeller
United States

Known for making people laugh, telling jokes, and being the life of the party, it has long been documented that when Fuzzy Zoeller walks into a room, the party starts. Fuzzy has always been a gallery favorite because of his interactive and endearing relationship with spectators. Fuzzy is one of only three golfers to have won the Masters in his first appearance in the event.

FAVORITE DRINK

"Fuzzy Vodka and tonic with a lime is my favorite drink," Zoeller said. "A friend asked me what I was going to do when golf slowed down and suggested I do a wine label. There were already a number of golfers with wine labels and I have always been a vodka drinker. I decided to create vodka and worked with a distiller in Bend, Oregon. I spent nearly four years creating vodka that I thought was really great. Fuzzy's Ultra-Premium Vodka is filtered ten times through charcoal and crushed volcanic rock before being blended with Cascade Mountain water and bottled at eighty proof. I am proud to say it was awarded a gold medal and a ninety-four rating from the Beverage Testing Institute."

19TH HOLE

Fuzzy enjoys spending time at the two courses he owns; the Covered Bridge Golf Club in Sellersburg, Indiana, and the Champions

Pointe Golf Club in Memphis, Indiana. "These courses are close to my hometown so I always nice to see familiar friends and faces when I go there," Zoeller said.

"My most memorable celebration was after I won the Masters in 1979. Going back to the clubhouse and having dinner with family and friends. Winning the Masters the first time ever appearing there was very special and it made the celebration even more spectacular because my mom, Alma, and dad, Frank, were there with me. The next year when I got to choose the menu for the Champions Dinner, White Castle cheeseburgers were served."

HOLES IN ONE

Fuzzy Zoeller has made eighteen holes in one. "The hole in one I made at Glen Oaks Country Club during the Allianz Championship was pretty spectacular," he said. "It is a one hundred and seventy-yard par three, the sixteenth hole at Glen Oaks Country Club. It landed in the rough and took a little bit before it rolled into the cup. It is one of the most watched hole-in-one videos on YouTube. I did not buy the clubhouse a round because it was during a tournament and I told the guys they should be buying *me* drinks. So they started giving me money and the next thing I knew I had three thousand and eight hundred dollars."

Arjun Atwal
India

With his 2010 win at the Wyndham Championship at Sedgefield Country Club in Greensboro, North Carolina, Arjun Atwal became the first golfer born in India to become a member of, and later win, on the PGA Tour. Originally from Calcutta, Atwal took up golf at the age of fourteen and came to the United States when he was sixteen years old. He began playing golf at the Royal Calcutta Golf Club in Kolkata, India, a club established in 1829, the oldest golf club in India and the first outside Great Britain.

"My win [at the Wyndham] was a huge deal in India," Atwal said. "My mother said it was all over the news and in the papers. It made me very proud and my family is very proud as well. It is a great feeling.

FAVORITE DRINK

"Tea is big in India because the English brought it over and the custom still exists," Atwal said. "It is a ritual as much as a drink. I drink tea two times every day in the morning and late afternoon, no matter where I am. My favorite drink is Johnny Walker Blue, especially after a win. This is the most famous scotch in India.

19TH HOLE

"My favorite grill room is the Isleworth Champions Grill. This is my home course and where I live with my family. The food is amazing

TWO GOOD ROUNDS

and they literally can make you whatever you want. I enjoy the fish tacos and a salad that they make for me with everything I like in it."

Atwal has made eight holes in one. "At the Canadian Open in 2009 I made a hole in one and won a car. It was at the Glen Abbey Golf Course in Oakville, Ontario, on the fourteenth hole—a par three.

HOLES IN ONE

"I remember making my first hole in one when I was fourteen or fifteen in India at the Royal Calcutta Golf Club. It was a great moment."

Don't Mess With Atwal's Balls

"When I was growing up in India, golf balls were very, very hard to come by, so you would never lose them," Atwal said. "To this day I am very possessive about my golf balls, even though I get them for free."

Like many other Tour pros, Arjun Atwal plays Titleist.

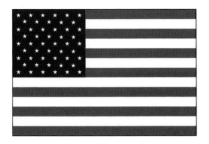

Boo Weekley
United States

Thomas Brent "Boo" Weekley's nickname comes from Yogi Bear's sidekick, Boo-Boo Bear. Boo is known for his Southern roots and his outdoor interests apart from golf such as hunting. Boo has his own line of camouflage-inspired golf clothing that reflects his outdoor nature, "Boo by Firethorn Tour."

Boo notes that after a round of golf he enjoys a natural light beer, especially in the summer. However if it is after a tournament he prefers a Crown Royal and water.

FAVORITE DRINK

Boo and I at the MasterCard tent during Playoffs- Deutsche Bank Championship

19TH HOLE　"My three favorite grill rooms are the TPC Sawgrass in Ponte Vedra, Florida, the Hilton Head Harbour Town at the Sea Pines Resort in South Carolina, and growing up the course that I played then, the Tanglewood Golf and Country Club in Milton, Florida. When I was playing there growing up there was only a snack bar and you brought your own cold beer."

After his win at the 2007 Verizon Heritage in Hilton Head Island, South Carolina, he stayed in the locker room buying drinks and hanging out with the volunteers and maintenance folks.

HOLES IN ONE　Weekley has made nine holes in one. "My first was great because it was at Tanglewood Golf Club in Milton, Florida, on the fifth hole by my Ma and Pa's house," he said.

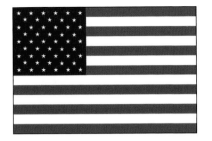

Cristie Kerr
United States

Cristie Kerr has fourteen wins on the LPGA Tour including two major championships. She was the number-one-ranked golfer in the Women's World Golf Rankings three times in 2010.

"I really enjoy red wine from Napa Valley, California," Kerr said. "When I am having a cocktail I like to have extra-dry double-cross vodka martini with blue-cheese olives."

FAVORITE DRINK

Celebrating her victory at the 2007 LPGA Championship

Kerr's wine label, Curvature, is a unique collaboration with Suzanne Pride Bryan, the owner of Pride Mountain Vineyards in St. Helena, California. Suzanne is a breast cancer survivor and Kerr is actively involved in fundraising for breast cancer research. Birdies for Breast Cancer is the foundation Kerr created in 2003, the year that her mother Linda was diagnosed with breast cancer. Curvature is a Cabernet Sauvignon and speaks to the passion of these extraordinary women with proceeds going to breast cancer research.

19TH HOLE "My favorite grill room is the Taproom at Pebble Beach," Kerr said. "I went on vacation with my husband there and it's the best!"

HOLES IN ONE "I have made a few holes in one," Kerr said. "One was during tournament competition in Korea. I also made one during a pro-am the next week in Japan and one at my home club in Mirabel in Arizona. There weren't too many people around [to witness them], sadly. The club gave me an etched hole-in-one bottle and delicious snacks!"

Jhonattan Vegas
Venezuela

In 2011, Vegas won his first PGA Tour event, the Bob Hope Classic. The victory was the first by a Venezuelan at a PGA Tour event and it also assured Vegas entry into the Masters. Vegas was born in Maturín, Venezuela, and played college golf at the University of Texas.

FAVORITE DRINK

"Johnny Vegas," as Jhonattan has been named by the press, favors an Arnold Palmer as his drink of choice after a round. He was introduced to it by some American friends at a golf club in Houston, Texas, and immediately took to it. When asked if it helps him channel his inner golf he laughs. "Well I don't know about that but I do enjoy the drink," he said. "In Venezuela in general we do not have a drink specific to Venezuela. Most people drink a lot of natural juices. Whiskey is very popular. I am not a big drinker, however sometimes I enjoy drinking a Polar or San Miguel beer with my friends after a round.

19TH HOLE

"In Venezuela we do not have this custom to spend a lot of time at the bar after a round. I rarely go to the 19th hole and have drinks. Usually we would go to a restaurant near the course but not necessarily spend time at the clubhouse. Some of my favorite 19th hole moments would be in 2000 after we won the Los Andes Cup, a

prestigious tournament in South America. It was held at the Guata-
paro Golf Club in Valencia, Venezuela, and I remember jumping into
the clubhouse pool with the captain. Also after I won the Argentine
Open I took a couple of sips of Champagne from the trophy cup on
the eighteenth hole after we won.

HOLES IN ONE Vegas has had two holes in one. He laughs and feels fortunate to
have gotten out of the responsibility of buying friends drinks afterwards. "We do have the custom to buy the clubhouse a round of
drinks [after a hole in one] but I got out of it both times, fortunately.
My first was during a practice round at Cypress Wood in Houston
on the third hole and I was not twenty-one yet. The second was
in Athens, Georgia, in 2009 during a Nationwide event on the thirteenth hole. It was during the tournament, so I did not buy drinks."

JHONATTAN VEGAS

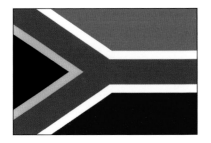

David Frost
South Africa

David Frost and his family have been in the wine business in South Africa for over sixty years. His father's vineyard was the first place Frost hit balls and the pocket money he made from picking grapes funded his first set of clubs and an ongoing supply of golf balls.

FAVORITE DRINK

"Growing up, playing as a junior, the best drink was a brown cow," Frost says. "That is a Coke with milk. Some guys liked the white cow, which is a ginger beer and milk. Those both still have good memories for me. Now that I am older, my favorite drink is a chilled Sauvignon Blanc from David Frost wines."

19TH HOLE

"My introduction to golf was to caddy for my dad on a Saturday afternoon at our home club, Stellenbosch, South Africa," Frost said. "When my dad was done playing he would go in the clubhouse bar and meet with friends. While he was in the clubhouse's 19th hole my brother and I would play the last three holes, which surrounded the clubhouse. In summer the days were longer and we could play the seventh, eighth and nineth holes, a par three, par five, and par three. We could play at least nine holes. We would check in after three holes to see if the old man was ready, [and] most of the time [he was] not since this was the place to have drinks. So for this reason the 19th hole at Stellenbosch is my favorite 19th hole. If it was not for this I might not have had my introduction to golf."

HOLES IN ONE   Frost has made four holes in one, all of them in tournaments. "One at the Tuckaway Country Club in Milwaukee on the eighth hole using a 6-iron, one in Sun City, South Africa, on the fourth hole using a 6-iron, in Portugal two hundred and thirty-five yards using a 5-iron," Frost said.

"A great moment was during the Presidents Cup in 1996 at the Robert Trent Jones Golf Club in Gainesville, Virginia. I used a 4-iron and hit it two hundred and eleven yards on the fourth hole for a hole in one.

"I did not make any [holes in one] as an amateur and luckily for me the pros never end up in the clubhouse for drinks afterwards. If they did I would pour them some wine from my winery. Frost wine!"

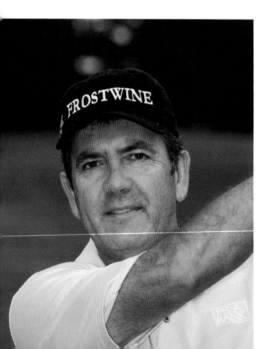

DAVID FROST

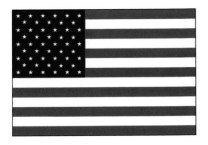

Nancy Lopez
United States

Nancy Lopez won 48 LPGA events in her career, including three majors. Four times she was named the LPGA Player of the Year and was named the Female Athlete of the Year twice by the Associated Press. She was inducted into the World Golf Hall of Fame in 1987.

FAVORITE DRINK

Nancy Lopez's favorite drink is milk. "I love milk," she said. "My father thought it was good for me and I always had a glass of milk before bed. One night before I went to bed I said, 'Dad, I can't breathe. I need milk.' And he ran out and got it. When I was at Tulsa on the golf team we would reward someone if they got up and down out of the bunker. Usually someone would buy the person a beer if they made it but other women knew I did not drink so they would always buy me milk.

19TH HOLE

"My favorite place would be Lopez Legacy Restaurant at the Villages in Florida," Lopez said. "I designed the twenty-seven-hole golf course there and all the holes are named after my daughters.

"A nice memory I have of a celebration was in 1981 when I won the Nabisco Dinah Shore Tournament at Million Hill Country Club in Palm Springs, California. We celebrated in the clubhouse but the victory was super because I got a lot of birdies—eight or nine on the last day. My dad and sister like beer and they were together walking the course and my dad came up to me after one of the birdies and said, 'Nancy, I drink to that birdie.' He would take a sip after each birdie.

"I grew up playing at the municipal golf course in Roswell, New Mexico. I have fond memories of spending time in the clubhouse after playing a round of golf with my mom and dad. I went to Goddard High School and played on the boys' golf team because they did not have a girls' team. I was the first girl to do that, and I remember we would carry our golf bags and the boys would put tee markers in my bag to make it heavy.

"Sometimes golfers drink alcohol out of the trophy cup after they win. I never did that. I never drank milk out of a trophy cup but I wish I had."

HOLES IN ONE Lopez has made nine holes in one, three as a pro and six as an amateur. "The most memorable was when I played in a senior event with Miller Barber in Montego Bay, Jamaica, and as a result of getting a hole in one I won a Mazda RX-7," she said. She has never bought a clubhouse a drink.

NANCY LOPEZ

Luke Donald
England

"I enjoy a Corona when I am relaxing and when I am not drinking my wine," Donald said. "I enjoy the Bordeaux-style wines. I ended up doing a wine label as a result of my friendship with Bill Terlato of Terlato wineries. We play golf together and we joke because he is an amateur golfer and I am an amateur wine maker. He helps me with wine and I help him with golf.

"My favorite 19th hole is my kitchen," Donald said. "After a tournament on Sunday I enjoy having a glass of wine in my house with my wife and daughter. Sunday is the beginning of my weekend as Monday is my day off.

"I really had a good time and a bit of a party after the Ryder Cup win in 2010," Donald continued. "Graeme McDowell, Rory McIlroy, and I did Jagerbombs. I also had a really nice time with friends after winning the BMW PGA Championship at Wentworth. By winning that tournament I became the number-one-ranked player in the world. A lot of my friends were there that I have known since I was twelve years old, so we all got together after the tournament at the hotel and had champagne. It was really nice to share that moment with them."

HOLES IN ONE

Donald has made eleven holes in one. "I have a few special holes in one," he said. "My first was at Hazlemere Golf Club, Buckinghamshire, England, when I was fourteen and it was a par-four, three hundred and thirty yards downhill. Another was during a tournament at Wentworth in England on the second hole. I also got a hole in one on the same hole on two different occasions, the third hole at Stoke Park country club in Buckinghamshire, England.

"Recently I got one while playing with Bill Terlato and Michael Jordan at the Bob O'Link Golf Club in Highland Park, IL. After the round I offered to buy drinks but they wouldn't let me."

Stoke Park Country Club and Resort

As a film location, Stoke Park has played host to the most memorable game of golf in cinema history, when James Bond defeated Auric Goldfinger on the eighteenth green in *Goldfinger* (1964). Goldfinger was the first of two James Bond films to be shot at Stoke Park, the second being *Tomorrow Never Dies* (1997).

LUKE DONALD

Matt Kuchar
United States

"I really enjoy a root beer float," Kuchar said. "It makes me feel like a kid. The combination of soda and ice cream—who doesn't love that? When I have something a little stronger I like Ketel One Tee Time. It is like an Arnold Palmer with vodka. I went to one of their events and they were making them. They are pretty good.

FAVORITE DRINK

"The Sea Island lodge would be my favorite 19th hole," Kuchar said. "It is comfortable, fun, and a really beautiful place.

19TH HOLE

"A great 19th hole memory is when I played the Masters in 1998, for the first time, and my Dad caddied for me. I got in as the low amateur. On Sunday after the tournament there is a Championship dinner and my mom, dad, sister, and grandparents all got to go.

"A favorite spot and something I look forward to every year is a house my dad's side of the family has on the lake in New Hampshire. Four generations of Kuchar's go there and it is very nice to sit around and get together with everyone."

Kuchar has made eight holes in one. "My most memorable [hole in one] was during the Wednesday Pro Am of a Nationwide event in Omaha," he said. Our foursome started on the tenth hole. So I was

HOLES IN ONE

on my seventeenth hole of the day, the eighth hole on the course, and I got a hole in one. I was eleven under for the day and all I had to do was birdie the next hole—my last hole of the round—for a score of fifty-nine and they blew the horn to stop play for the day. There were still two groups ahead trying to finish their round so we just stopped and I still ended on a high note with a hole in one. It was exciting and the guys I was playing with were going nuts.

"The hole in one was during competition so there are free drinks in the clubhouse anyway. That was an extra bonus."

2010 Barclays Champion Kuchar in the press room

TWO GOOD ROUNDS

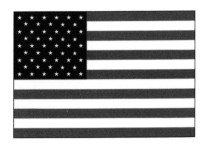

Keegan Bradley
United States

"Diet Coke is my favorite drink. When I am relaxing with friends or after golf I enjoy a Stella [Artois] beer. There might have been some Stella in the PGA Wannamaker Trophy Sunday after the win. There were a few cold ones in there for sure."

19TH HOLE

"The Grouper in Jupiter, Florida, is my 19th hole," Bradley said. "The best thing about winning the [2011] PGA Championship was when I took the Wannamaker Trophy on a local tour of Jupiter, Florida, for a few days. I really wanted to have the people that may not have access to the Trophy to touch it, to hold it, to grab it. After the Bruins won the Stanley Cup, a defenseman grabbed the Stanley Cup, walked out of his house in Boston and walked around the street with the Cup, and just had people touch it. I thought that was the coolest thing. So I wanted people to touch it and hold it and the look on their faces was like they were looking at a ghost or something. It was really fun."

19TH HOLE

Bradley has made two holes in one. "The first was the most memorable," he said. "I was in college at St. John's at the time and play-

HOLES IN ONE

The 2011 PGA Championship winner and I at the Barclays

TWO GOOD ROUNDS

ing in a tournament at Bethpage Red and my mom was on the green. It was a really good feeling. I was underage at the time, so I escaped buying drinks."

Champion to Champion

"I am a huge Boston sports fan," Bradley said. "When I am not wearing my Cleveland visor I have my Red Sox hat on. Tuesday after the PGA Championship win I woke up and I had a text from Tom Brady, my absolute hero. I almost thought of just keeping it to myself and not telling anyone because that is how much Tom Brady means to me and my career. To get a text from him reaching out to me was a highlight of my career."

New England Patriots quarterback Tom Brady at Pebble Beach

Epilogue:
A Tribute to Seve Ballesteros

Known for being wild and free, Seve Ballesteros played his heart out on the golf course. There was no other way for him. He was someone who taught those around him to enjoy life, laugh, live passionately, and reach high. I am blessed

to have known him. Seve was a sportsman, a public figure, father, husband, brother, and friend to many, and he came into our lives for a reason, a season, a lifetime.

Upon presenting Seve with the lifetime achievement award in 2009, fellow Spaniard José María Olazábal said this of his good friend: "I met you when I was fifteen; since then we have been through a lot. You belong to a group of golf professionals that changed the image of the game of golf all around the world. Your achievements speak for themselves, five majors and over seventy tournament wins. It is not just those achievements that make you special. More so it is the way you did it. You did it with a lot of imagination, lots of skills, but most important, you did it with all your heart. I know that because I have had the privilege to be close to you in some of those occasions. You were the first one to play the game of golf with such desire and passion and by doing so you made a lot of us believe that it was possible to achieve those goals."

Salud, Amor y Dinero y tiempo para hacerlo
(To health, love and wealth and time to enjoy it)
A Spanish saying used while toasting

Acknowledgments

Thanks, Gracias, Domo arigato, Merci, Kamsahamnida, Vinaka, Tika hoki, Dankie, Grazie, Go raibh maith agat, Tack, Danke schön, Tapadh leat, Dhanyawaad:

To the millions of golf fans around the globe that watch and play golf each week.

A very special heartfelt thank you to the players and the agents that worked with me on this book and to the Skyhorse Publishing team, especially Tony Lyons and Mark Weinstein.

Words cannot fully express my gratitude for the special people in my life that I am privileged to call friends and family, the ones closest to the sun. Your support and unwavering belief that this and other projects would come to fruition means the world to me and for that I am eternally grateful. You make me believe I can fly. Thank you for being the special people you are: Johnny Rhodes, Diane Curtin, Brigitte Adams, Claire Wexler, Greg Bryan, Vern McMillan, and especially Paul Bader for your support and encouragement.

About the Author

Elisa Gaudet has spent the past several years working in the golf industry in the U.S. and Latin America. She worked for the PGA Tour and the Tour de las Américas before founding Executive Golf International (www.execgolfintl.com) in 2003, a strategic golf marketing firm that works with clients to develop and implement golf related programs. Prior to golf Elisa worked in the entertainment industry for over 10 years as a model and SAG and AFTRA actress. She has appeared on numerous radio and TV programs and has been a guest speaker on a variety of golf topics. She has written several golf related articles and her syndicated "On the Lip" (www.onthelip.com) column has been running since 2003. In 2011 she launched the Two Good Rounds brand (www.twogoodrounds.com). She splits her time between New York City and Palm Beach, Florida.

Served at the
Hollywood Home of
Mr. and Mrs. Bob Hope

WHEN *YOU* and BOB HOPE *RELAX* . . .

WHETHER you shoot golf in the low 70's, like Bob "Hole-in-One" Hope, or celebrate when you break 100, you'll find Pabst Blue Ribbon Beer is always a pleasant, friendly companion.

That ever-faithful, *real beer flavor* you enjoy in Pabst Blue Ribbon

was achieved by 104 years of pioneering in the *Art of Brewing* . . . and the *Science of Blending*.

By tasting, by comparing, you will understand why millions have settled down to the real beer enjoyment that comes with blended, splendid Pabst Blue Ribbon.

Pabst
Blue Ribbon

33 FINE BREWS BLENDED INTO ONE GREAT BEER

With the Great Jack Nicklaus at the Masters

With 1973 U.S. Open champion Johnny Miller and 2004 U.S. Senior Open Champion Peter Jacobsen

With 1991 PGA and 1995 British Open champion John Daly

Ryuji Imada, Ernie Els and Stuart Appleby all have interesting headcovers in their bags, but their bags are not equipped with cup holders.

My Favorite 19th Hole Memories